Tide pools contain mysterious worlds,
where all the beauty of the sea
is subtly suggested and
portrayed in miniature.

—RACHEL CARSON

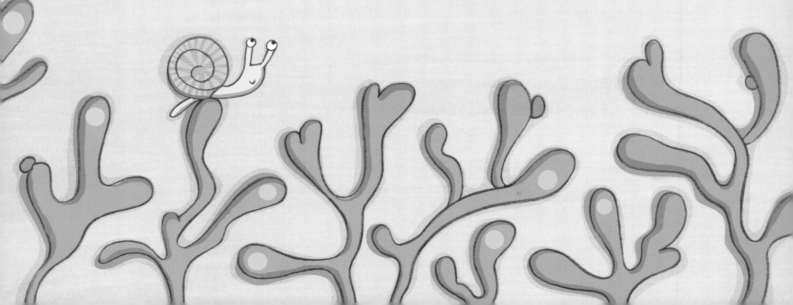

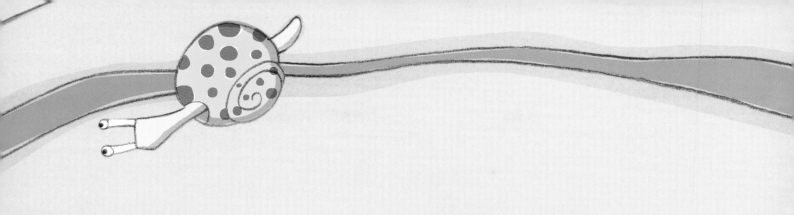

# OCEAN SOUP

## Tide-Pool Poems

Stephen R. Swinburne

*Illustrated by* **Mary Peterson**

**Charlesbridge**

# The Soup That Bites

Tide-pool soup is really good,
a most delicious snack.
But careful! When you take a bite,
this soup might bite you back.
Crabs will pinch and urchins poke.
It's rough out there—no joke!

## TIDE POOLS

Tide-pool animals have developed ways to survive the daily changes in
their habitat. Barnacles and mussels shut tight when exposed to air
and hot sun, keeping them moist inside their shells. Starfish, crabs,
and small fish seek shelter under damp rocks or wet seaweed.

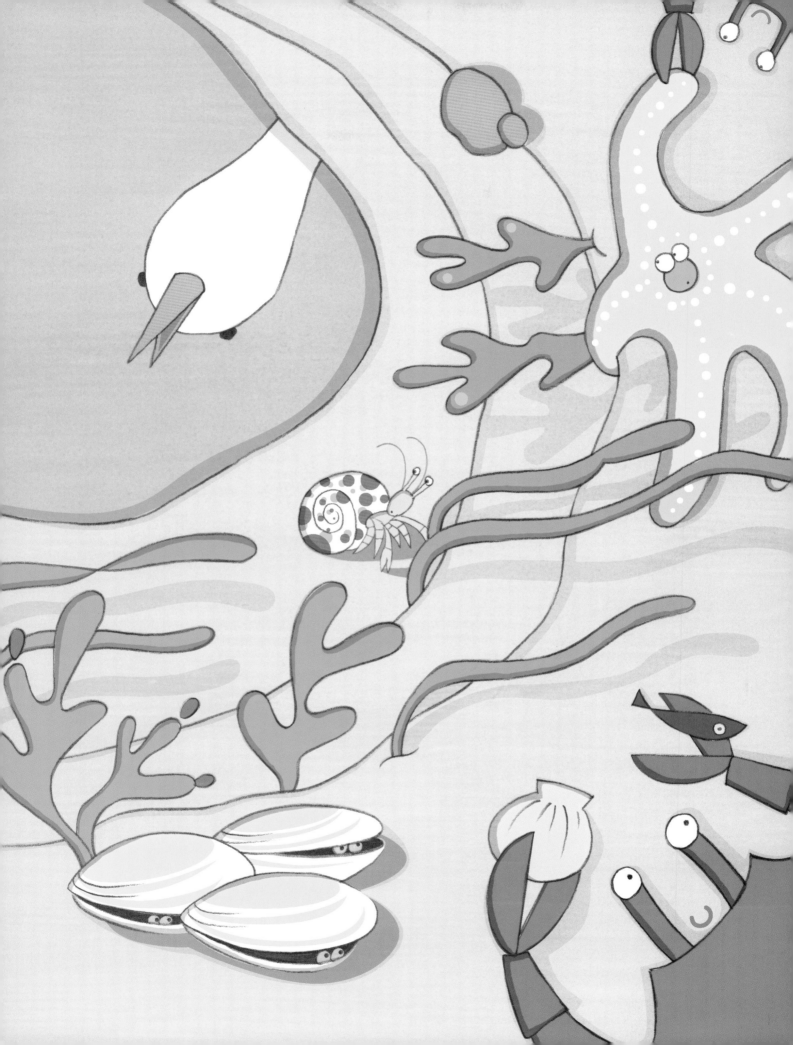

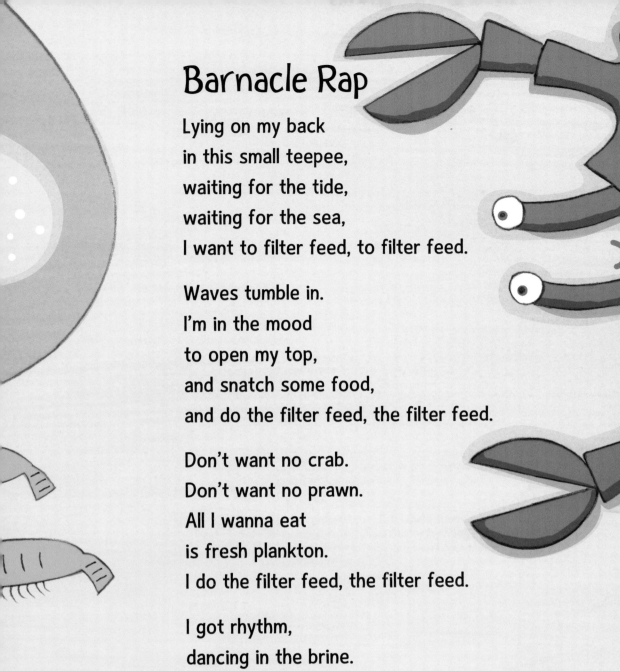

# Barnacle Rap

Lying on my back
in this small teepee,
waiting for the tide,
waiting for the sea,
I want to filter feed, to filter feed.

Waves tumble in.
I'm in the mood
to open my top,
and snatch some food,
and do the filter feed, the filter feed.

Don't want no crab.
Don't want no prawn.
All I wanna eat
is fresh plankton.
I do the filter feed, the filter feed.

I got rhythm,
dancing in the brine.
Life as a barnacle
is so sublime.
I love the filter feed, the filter feed.

## BARNACLES

Barnacles are related to crabs, shrimp, and lobsters.
What does a barnacle look like inside its little, white
home? Imagine a tiny, shrimplike creature with its head
stuck to the floor, kicking food into its mouth with
its legs. Barnacles fasten themselves to any surface:
rocks, pilings, boats—even whales and sea turtles.

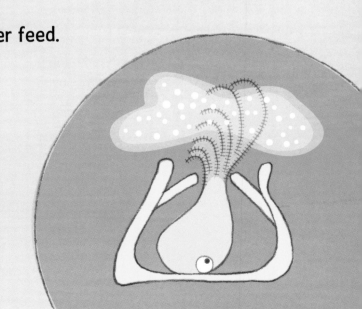

# Hairy Doris

Hello, my name is Doris.
I'm a shell-less gastropod,
but you can call me "sea slug,"
if gastropod sounds odd.

Don't you think I'm gorgeous?
With my raspy tongue I scrape
for bits of healthy food to eat.
A slug must watch her shape.

I'm really rather lucky that
I have no pesky shell.
Behold my lovely body—
I'm a stunning tide-pool belle!

Hello, my name is Doris.
I'm a shell-less gastropod,
but you can call me "sea slug,"
if gastropod sounds odd.

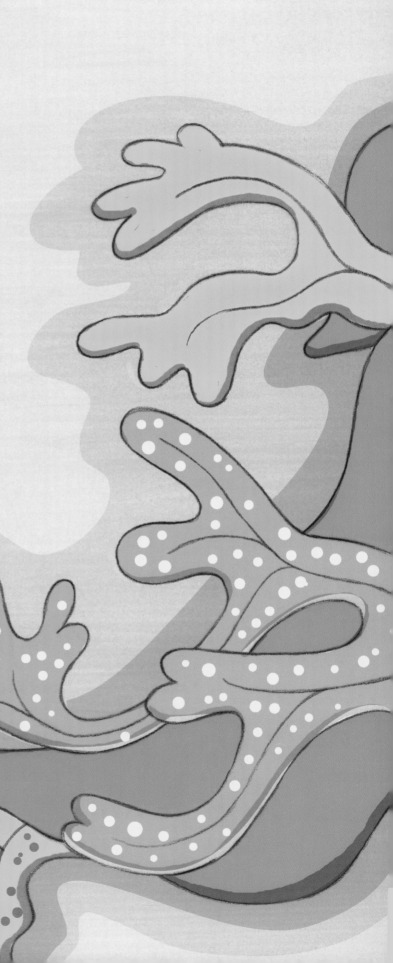

## SEA SLUGS

Sea slugs use tentacles on their heads to smell and touch.
They eat plants or small animals by scraping them off rocks
and seaweed with their tongues. The jellylike bodies of marine
sea slugs vary in color more than those of garden slugs.

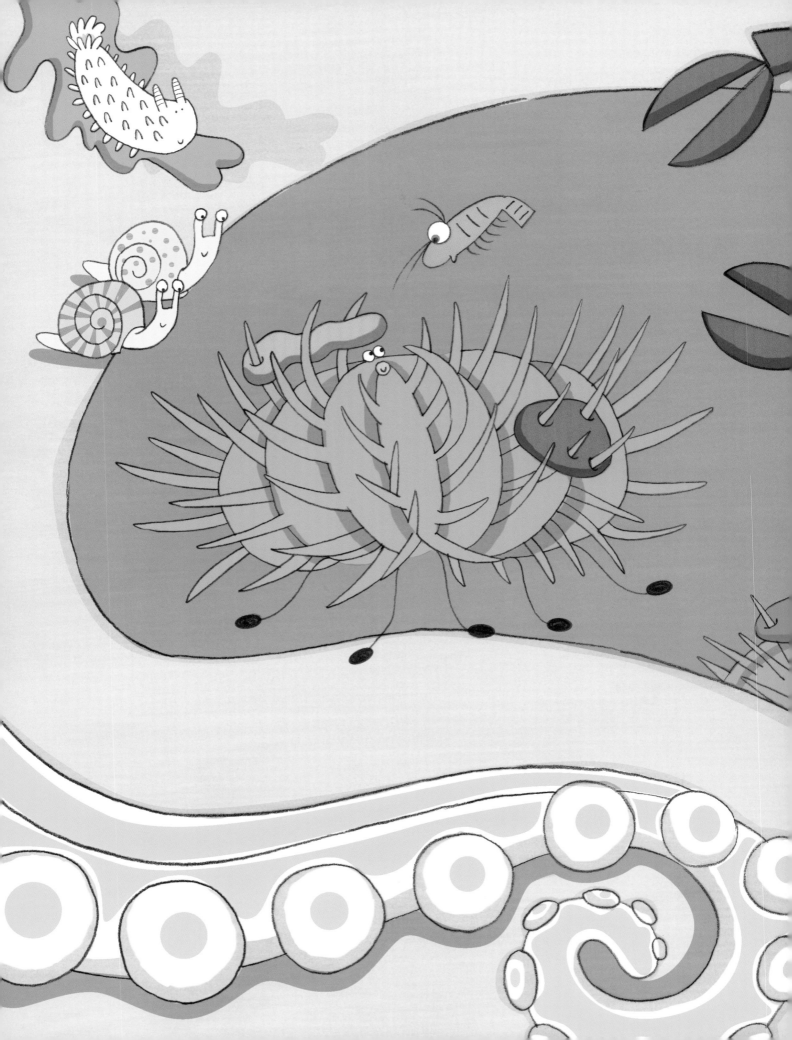

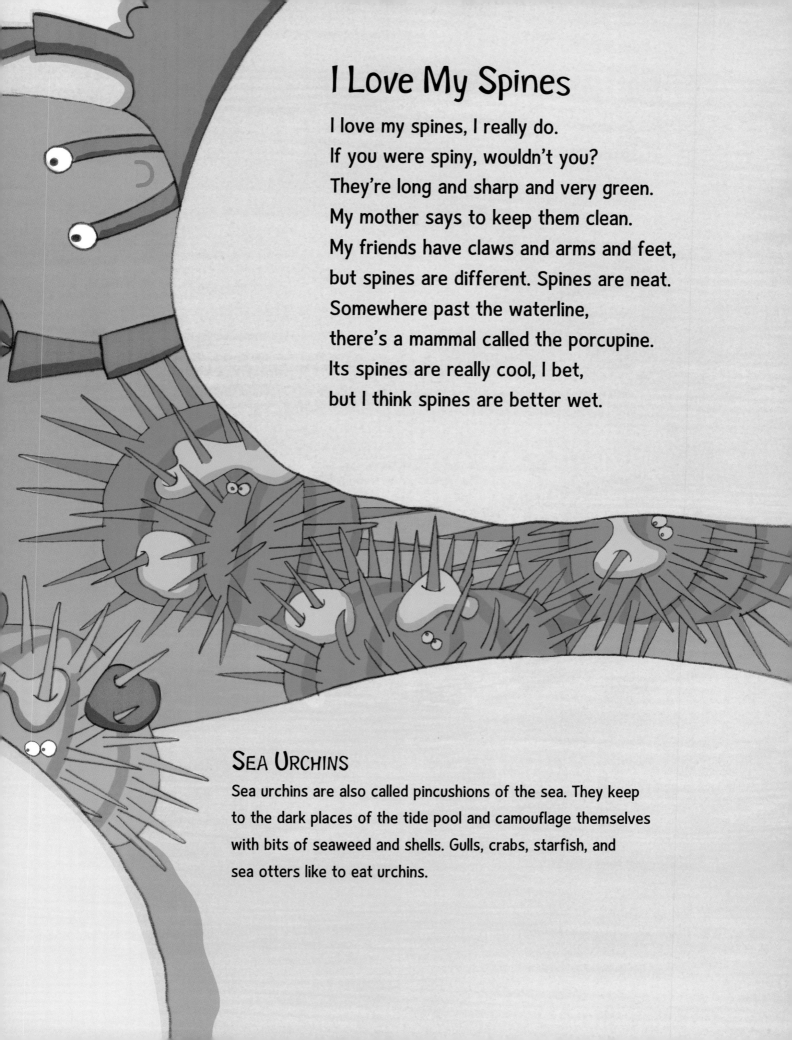

# I Love My Spines

I love my spines, I really do.
If you were spiny, wouldn't you?
They're long and sharp and very green.
My mother says to keep them clean.
My friends have claws and arms and feet,
but spines are different. Spines are neat.
Somewhere past the waterline,
there's a mammal called the porcupine.
Its spines are really cool, I bet,
but I think spines are better wet.

## SEA URCHINS

Sea urchins are also called pincushions of the sea. They keep
to the dark places of the tide pool and camouflage themselves
with bits of seaweed and shells. Gulls, crabs, starfish, and
sea otters like to eat urchins.

# Old, Cold Fish

Hello, little shrimp.
I need a better look.
I'm an old, cold fish with bulgy eyes,
living in this nook.

Swim closer if you will.
It's hard for me to hear.
I'm an old, cold fish with bulgy eyes,
underneath this pier.

What was that you said?
Come whisper in my ear.
I'm an old, cold fish with bulgy eyes,
my charming shrimpy dear.

Yesssssssss, you're nice and close.
No need to look alarmed.
I'm an old, cold fish with bulgy eyes.
I'd *never* cause you harm.

You're tasty, little shrimp.
A yummy meal at that!
I'm an old, cold fish with bulgy eyes.
I'm glad we had this chat.

## SCULPINS

Sculpins have large, armored heads with sharp spines along the sides. These well-camouflaged fish lurk among rocks and seaweed. If small fish or shrimp come within striking distance, sculpins open their huge mouths like a trap. Water rushes in along with the victims.

# Move Over, Mussel

Move over, mussel—you're sitting on my thread.
How's a mussel s'posed to eat
in this overcrowded bed?

Move over, mussel—you know I got here first.
There are way too many mussels here.
This bed's about to burst!

Move over, mussel—you're getting in my face.
I'm putting down my foot.
I've got to leave this place.

Move over, mussel—it's time to relocate.
These mussels are too greedy
and much too overweight.

## MUSSELS

Mussels are filter feeders with two siphons, or tubes.
One tube sucks water and plankton in, and the other
spews water and waste out. Mussels filter about ten
to fifteen gallons of water per day. They anchor
themselves to tide-pool rocks with tough, sticky
threads made by a gland in their foot.

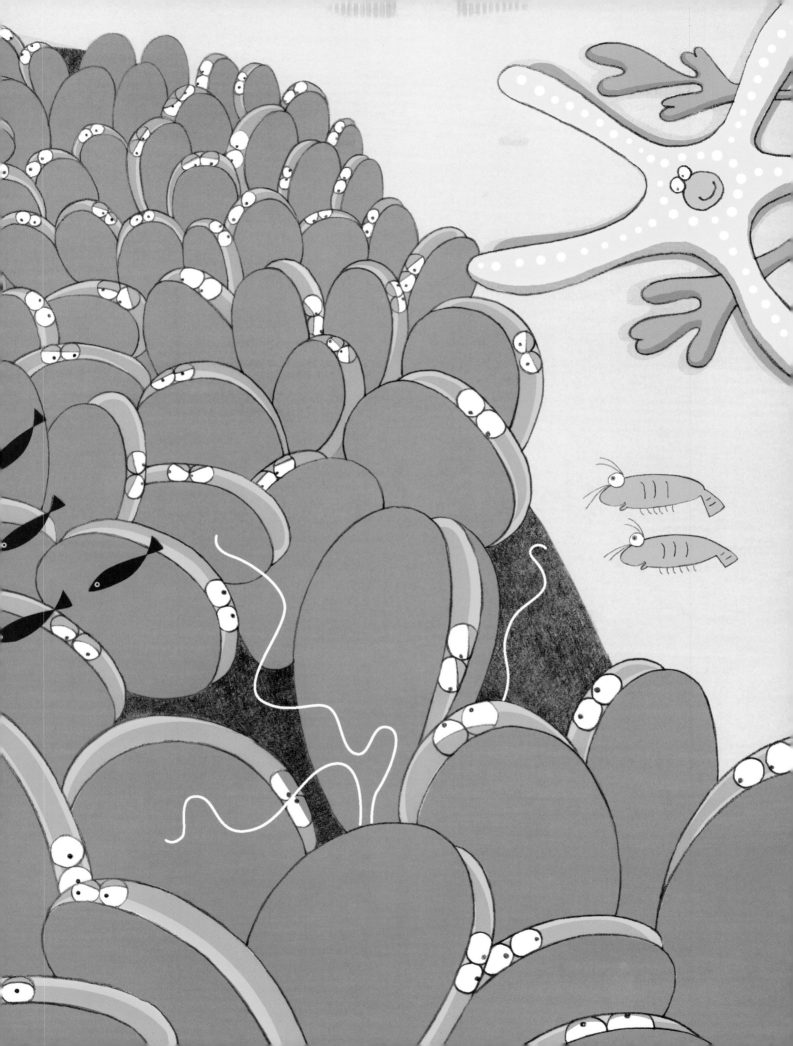

# Regenerate

In the tide pool where I dwell,
five arms grasp a mussel shell.
A crab comes—SNIP!—there goes my arm.
Rude, yes, but I'm not alarmed.
There won't be need to operate,
since starfish arms regenerate.

## STARFISH

Starfish, also called sea stars, are related to sea urchins. While urchins are vegetarians, starfish are aggressive carnivores. A starfish first wraps its arms around a mussel or clam. Then it wrenches open the shelled creature, slips its stomach inside the shell, and begins eating. Starfish have an amazing ability to regenerate—a whole new starfish can grow from just one arm and a small part of the body.

# Dome Home

I'm a hermit crab who needs a home.
I've got to find the perfect dome.
I'm looking for a carapace,
a nice, new shell with lots of space.
Scuttle to the left, scuttle to the right.
In my new shell, I'll scuttle all night.

A bigger shell would suit me more.
I'll search across this tide-pool floor.
Let's go crab-walk into town.
I'll keep my eyestalks looking down.
Scuttle to the left, scuttle to the right.
In my new shell, I'll scuttle all night.

Here's a shell a crab could love.
Hey, it fits me like a glove.
I wave my claws in celebration.
Look at me—a chic crustacean!
Scuttle to the left, scuttle to the right.
In my new shell, I'll scuttle all night.

## HERMIT CRABS

Hermit crabs are born without shells on their abdomens. They locate discarded shells from creatures such as whelks or moon snails and use them for protection. As hermit crabs' bodies grow, the crabs seek out larger and larger shells.

# Room with a View

I live in a room by the sea,
where the view is great and the food is free.
Some of the tenants come and go.
Some I eat, if they're too slow.
One end of me is firmly locked.
The other end just gently rocks.
I live in a room by the sea.
It's perfect for an anemone.

## ANEMONES

Sea anemones look like underwater flowers, but they are actually
carnivorous animals related to jellyfish. Anemone tentacles, like
those of the jellyfish, are armed with tiny poisonous sacs that
paralyze small fish on contact. The tentacles then contract,
drawing prey into the anemone's mouth.

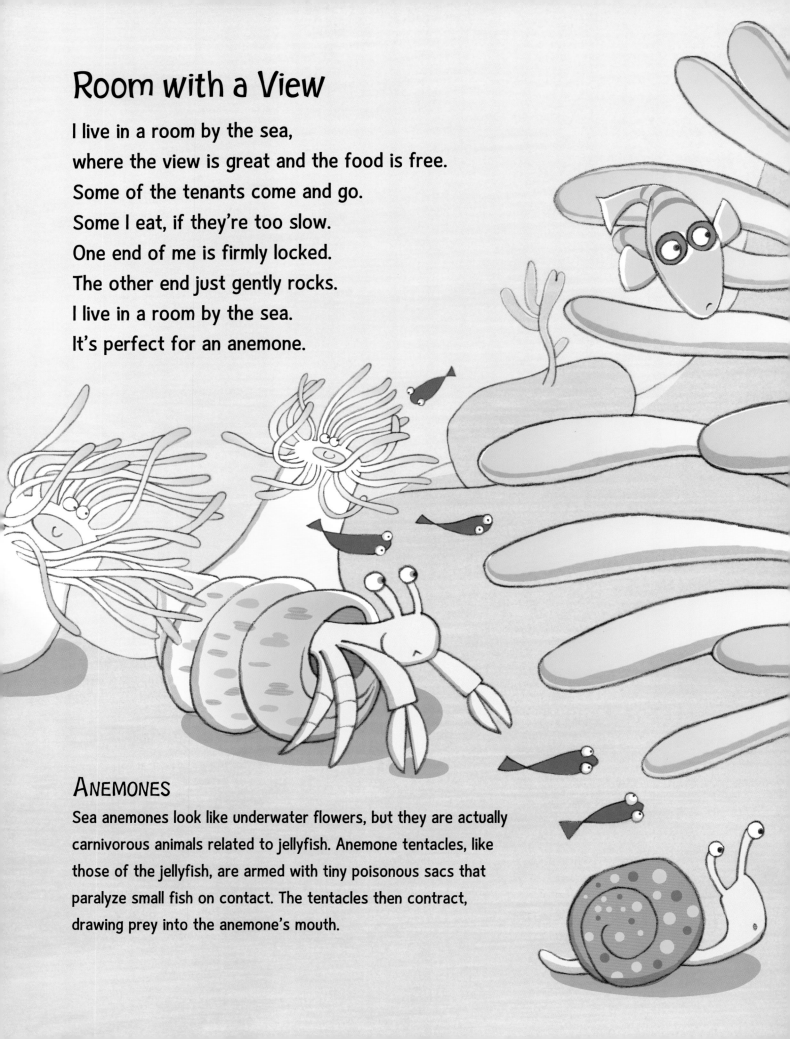

# Bully of the Tide

I'm a low-down, dirty lobster, bully of the tide.
You'd better keep your head down. You'd better run and hide.
Check out my huge thorax. Have you ever seen such claws?
I nosh on crabs and starfish. Clams I like to gnaw.
I hunt my food at nighttime. I like to dine alone.
I'll nibble on your babies. I'll eat you when full-grown.
I'm a low-down, dirty lobster, bully of the tide.
You'd better keep your head down. You'd better run and hide.

I'm a low-down, dirty lobster, bully of the tide.
You'd better run for cover, unless you want to die.
I'll crunch you when you're living. I'll scavenge your remains.
I'll suck up all your juices. I'll pick apart your brains.
I'm not big into veggies. Call me carnivore.
I find the meat I want to eat. It's all along the shore.
I'm a low-down, dirty lobster, bully of the tide.
You'd better keep your head down. You'd better run and hide.

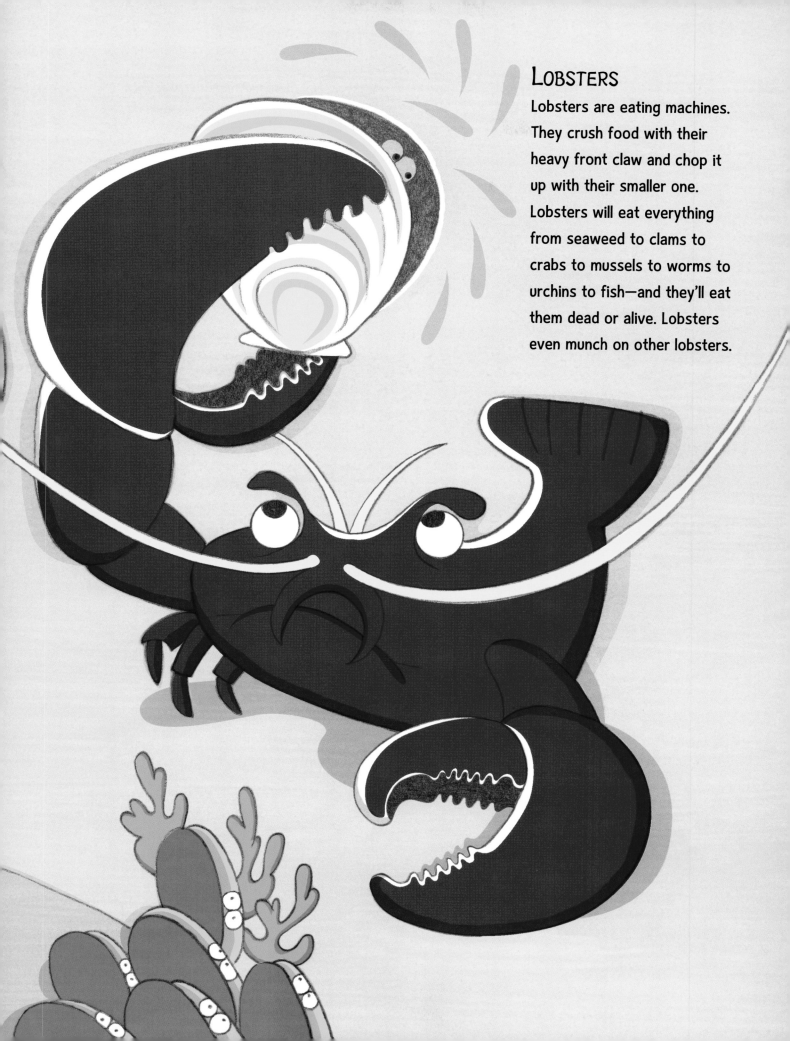

## LOBSTERS

Lobsters are eating machines. They crush food with their heavy front claw and chop it up with their smaller one. Lobsters will eat everything from seaweed to clams to crabs to mussels to worms to urchins to fish—and they'll eat them dead or alive. Lobsters even munch on other lobsters.

# A Starfish Interviews an Octopus

*Where are you, octopus?*

   Hiding in a crevice, trying to catch some z's,
   waiting to greet you with a saltwater squeeze.

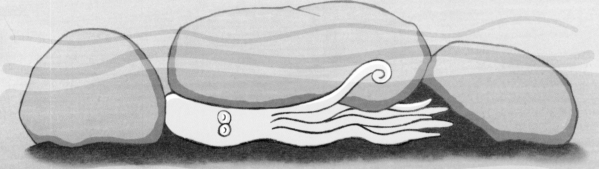

*I hear you have three hearts. Is that true?*

   Two hearts pump blood through each of my gills.
   A third pumps blood to keep away the chills.

*What do you eat?*

   I chomp on clams and crabs and fish.
   Snails and scallops make a very dainty dish.

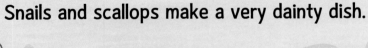

**How do you move?**

I creep, I crawl. I scuttle and slide.
Across the sand and rocks I glide.

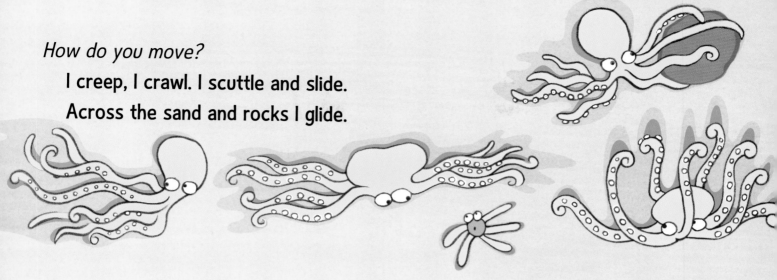

**Aren't you forgetting one other way you move?**

I squirt water from my funnel to help me jet away.
This skill helps me escape—and also gets me prey.

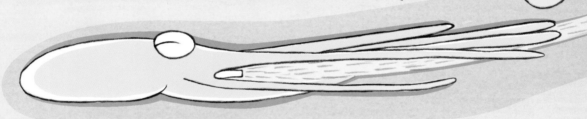

**Why are you looking at me like that, octopus?**

All this chatter made me hungry for meat.
You look so sweet—good enough to eat!

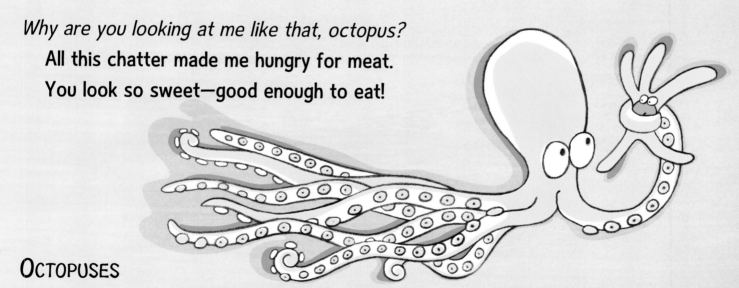

## OCTOPUSES

Octopuses come equipped with three hearts and hundreds of suckers
on their eight muscular arms. They also have a hard, parrotlike beak that
tears pieces of flesh from their prey. Octopuses don't have any bones,
and even a large octopus can squeeze into a hole the size of a quarter.

# Food in the Water

We hear the waves coming. They're not far away.
Our food's in the water, in the wet, wild spray.
We see the waves coming, foamy and white.
Our food's in the water. We'll soon take a bite.
We feel the waves coming, with a boom and a crash.
Our food's in the water, in the next ocean splash.
We taste the waves at last, all bubbly and cool.
Our food's in the water—we love our tide pool!

## PLANKTON

The ocean is filled with huge, drifting clouds of microscopic plants
and animals called plankton. Twice a day the tides rise and wash
over the rocky shore with a fresh plankton soup. Barnacles, clams,
mussels, and other filter feeders hungrily snatch and strain plankton
from the seawater. The incoming tide is so incredibly rich that a
drop of ocean contains thousands of plankton.

# GLOSSARY

**abdomen:** the hind end of a crustacean, containing the digestive and reproductive organs

**camouflage:** something that hides an animal by changing how it looks

**carapace:** a hard, protective outer shell

**carnivore:** an animal that eats other animals

**crustacean:** an aquatic animal with a hard outer shell and a three-part body: head, thorax, and abdomen (shrimp, crab, lobster, and barnacle)

**echinoderm:** a spiny-skinned animal (starfish and sea urchin)

**eyestalk:** a moveable column with an eye at the tip

**gastropod:** a type of mollusk, usually—but not always—with a distinct head and a spiral shell

**gland:** an organ that produces a liquid

**habitat:** an area or environment where animals and plants live

**invertebrate:** an animal with no backbone

**mollusk:** a soft-bodied invertebrate, usually enclosed in a hard shell (clam, mussel, snail, octopus, and sea slug)

**regeneration:** regrowing lost or destroyed parts of the body

**siphon:** a tube through which an animal sucks in or pushes out water

**tentacle:** a flexible limb that sticks out near an animal's head, usually used to feel

**thorax:** the middle section of the body of a crustacean, located between the head and the abdomen

# AUTHOR'S NOTE

Wanderers, swimmers, crawlers; snatchers, suckers, scrapers; hitchhikers, hangers-on, and hiders—tide pools support an amazing diversity of plants and animals. From the Arctic to Chesapeake Bay on the Atlantic coast and from Alaska to Mexico on the Pacific, North America is home to countless tide pools. This land-sea habitat is sustained and nourished by clean air and pure ocean waters. If we are willing to solve the threats of coastal development and ocean pollution that endanger tide-pool communities, this narrow ribbon of wilderness might remain undisturbed for generations to come.

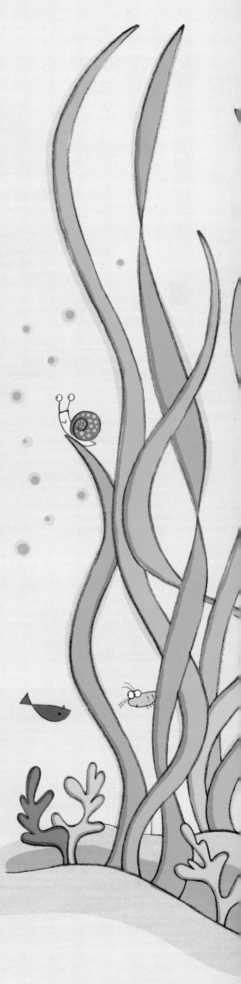

# RESOURCES

Bredeson, Carmen. *Tide Pools.* First Books. New York: Franklin Watts, 1999.

Brenner, Barbara. *One Small Place by the Sea.* New York: HarperCollins, 2004.

### Habitats—Tidepool

http://olympiccoast.noaa.gov/living/habitats/tidepool/welcome.html
Read about the climate, habitat, and residents of the Pacific Northwest's
tide-pool regions. Includes guidelines for visiting a tide pool.

Hunter, Anne. *What's in the Tide Pool?* Boston: Houghton Mifflin, 2000.

### Life on the Rocky Shore

http://library.thinkquest.org/J001418/
Learn about tide-pool animals, intertidal zones, and safety tips for visiting a tide pool.

### Monterey Bay Aquarium: Tide Pool Video

www.montereybayaquarium.org/efc/efc_rocky/rocky_cam.asp
See a video of a coastal tide pool at the Monterey Bay Aquarium and
use the tide-pool spotting guide to help identify animals in the video.
Includes a downloadable tide-pool etiquette guide.

### Secrets of the Tide Pools

http://library.thinkquest.org/J002608/Tidepool_home_page.html
Learn about tide pools of the Pacific coastline. Includes an explanation of the
three intertidal zones and the animals and plants that live within each zone.

Sexton, Colleen. *Tide Pools.* Blastoff! Readers. New York: Children's Press, 2008.

Silverstein, Alvin and Virginia B. *Life in a Tidal Pool.* Mineola, NY: Dover Publications, 2005.

Wright, Alexandra. *At Home in the Tide Pool.* Watertown, MA: Charlesbridge, 1992.

To my awesome and audacious uncle and aunt,
Bob and Cathy Swinburne, with all my love—S. R. S.

For Jenna, Petra, and Nigel—M. P.

The author wishes to thank Dr. Paul Loiselle of the New York Aquarium (www.nyaquarium.com)
and Don Riepe of the American Littoral Society (www.alsnyc.org) for reviewing the book.

Text copyright © 2010 by Stephen R. Swinburne
Illustrations copyright © 2010 by Mary Peterson

Published by Charlesbridge
85 Main Street
Watertown, MA 02472
(617) 926-0329
www.charlesbridge.com

Library of Congress Cataloging-in-Publication Data
Swinburne, Stephen R.
    Ocean soup : tide-pool poems / Stephen R. Swinburne ; illustrations by Mary Peterson.
        p. cm.
    ISBN 978-1-58089-200-1 (reinforced for library use)
    ISBN 978-1-58089-201-8 (softcover)
1. Tide pool animals—Juvenile literature.  I. Peterson, Mary. II. Title.
QL122.2.S95 2009
591.769'9—dc22                            2008026960

Printed in China
(hc) 10 9 8 7 6 5 4 3 2 1
(sc) 10 9 8 7 6 5 4 3 2 1

Illustrations done in pencil and painted in Adobe Photoshop and Adobe Illustrator
Display type and text type set in Ogre and Humper
Color separations by Chroma Graphics, Singapore
Printed and bound September 2009 in Nansha, Guangdong, China by Everbest Printing Company, Ltd.,
    through Four Colour Imports, Ltd., Louisville, Kentucky
Production supervision by Brian G. Walker
Designed by Martha MacLeod Sikkema

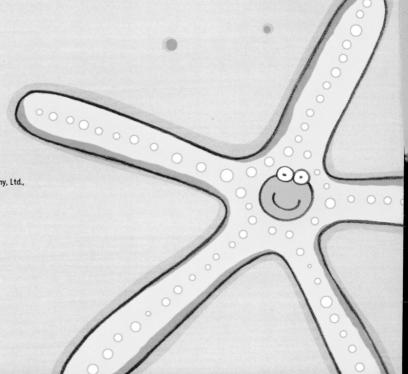